Parents Praise
What Will Bear, Rabbit, and Chipmunk Do Next?

"This story, and the idea of a wordless book, held my five-year-old's interest the entire time. The illustrations are beautiful. He was excited to interpret what happened next in his own words. This took away any frustration with learning to read and helped to build his confidence in reading!"
—Sarah Toy

"My son was proud of his accomplishment and the knowledge that others would read his work."
—Alison Kalil

"I loved watching my son figure out how the story was going to unfold. He took to it quickly and was able to retell the story over and over."
—Whitney Fancher

"This book was so fun for my children. I am amazed at the creativity it has sparked and the different stories they each created."
—Kelly Lippert

"This book is an engaging way to draw a reluctant writer into the writing process. They start writing a story without even realizing it!"
—Kristy Bachelor

"I LOVED watching Vera's creativity and imagination in writing a story all by herself. She was inspired to be an author!"
—Christina Willman

WORDLESS BOOKS FOR YOUNG AUTHORS

What Will Bear, Rabbit and Chipmunk Do Next?

Jim Chansler & Lyle Lee Jenkins

ISBN (paperback): 978-1-956457-62-9

Book design: Christy Day, Constellation Book Services
Publishing consultant: Martha Bullen, Bullen Publishing Services
Distribution Coordinator: Maggie McLaughlin

Printed in the United States of America

Look for current and future titles by Lyle Lee Jenkins within these series:

Bible Patterns for Young Readers
> *A Day with Jesus: The Story of Zacchaeus*
> *A Week with Joshua: The Battle of Jericho*
> *An Evening with Daniel: The Lions' Den Theatre*
> *Two Weeks with Paul: A Shipwreck*
> *Five Years Protecting Jesus: A Christmas Story*
> *Eight Days with Thomas: An Easter Story*
> *A Very Long Day with Elijah: The Contest*
> *An Exciting Night with Peter: A Jailbreak*
> *Three Days with Jonah: A Whale of a Story*

Aesop Patterns for Young Readers
> *Who's Afraid of a Lion? Aesop's Bully Fable*
> *Yummy, Yummy, Yummy, Honey, Honey, Honey:*
> > *Aesop's Groupthink Fable*
> *The Thirsty Crow: Aesop's Little by Little Fable*
> *Sour Grapes: Aesop's Fooling Yourself Fable*

Pattern Block Stories for Young Readers

Other books by Lyle Lee Jenkins:

> *How to Create a Perfect School*
> *How to Create a Perfect Home School*
> > *with Kelly Hawkinson Lippert*
> *Optimize Your School*
> *From Systems Thinking to Systemic Action*
> *All About Henry: Rich Widower of Savannah Valley*

To get the most from your **Wordless Book for Young Authors**, follow the directions below.

1. **Take a picture walk.** Upon first reading, children will naturally look at all the art. Encourage them to move slowly through the book and look at each picture. Ask them to make predictions about what they think is happening or will happen in the upcoming pages. Guide them in identifying the characters, setting, potential problems, and solutions as they move through the pages.

2. **Write your story.** The next step is for the children to dictate the words for each page of the book while an adult records the child's language. This can be written directly in the book or typed into a template for 3" x 7" labels. The art on each page is 7" x 7" leaving the space at the bottom of each page for writing. It is vital that adults write the child's language exactly how children dictate it. The magic of this process is in the child hearing their words read back to them, even if it goes against what an adult may think it should say.

The template for the labels looks like this:

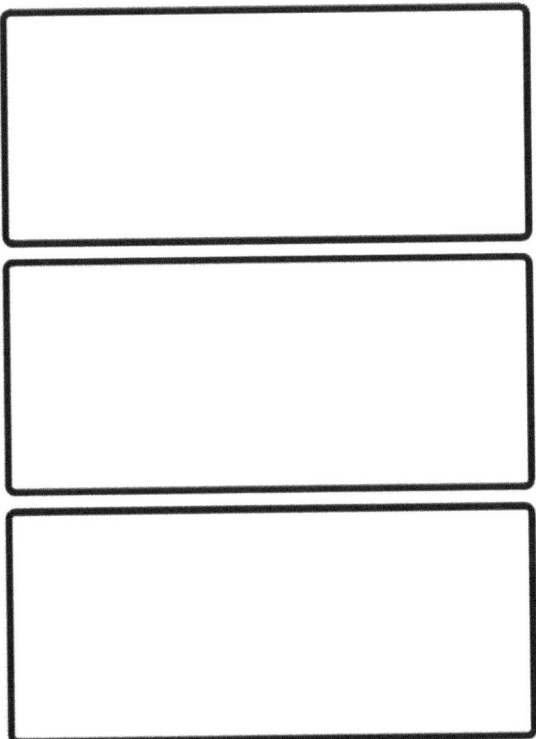

Three pages of dictated language can be printed on each sheet of the self-adhesive labels from Avery or other firms. There are more labels in the package than needed for this book. Hold on to them to use in other *Wordless Books for Young Authors*.

3. **Read your book.** Now it's time to read the finished product. Encourage children to read their book back to you or to friends and family. Your little author just wrote a book!

What Will Bear, Rabbit, and Chipmunk Do Next? may be the first book children will ever author and read out loud. Children will have favorite pages they can read quickly, and other pages that require practice. Soon they will be able to read the entire book! Fun for readers of all ages.

Many of the owners of this book may also have a copy of *Brown Bear, Brown Bear,* or other books by Bill Martin Jr. He taught his whole career that the most important reading skill for children is to know they can "make a go" of reading. Bear, rabbit, and chipmunk are ready to help thousands of children experience the joy of creating their own story and reading it.

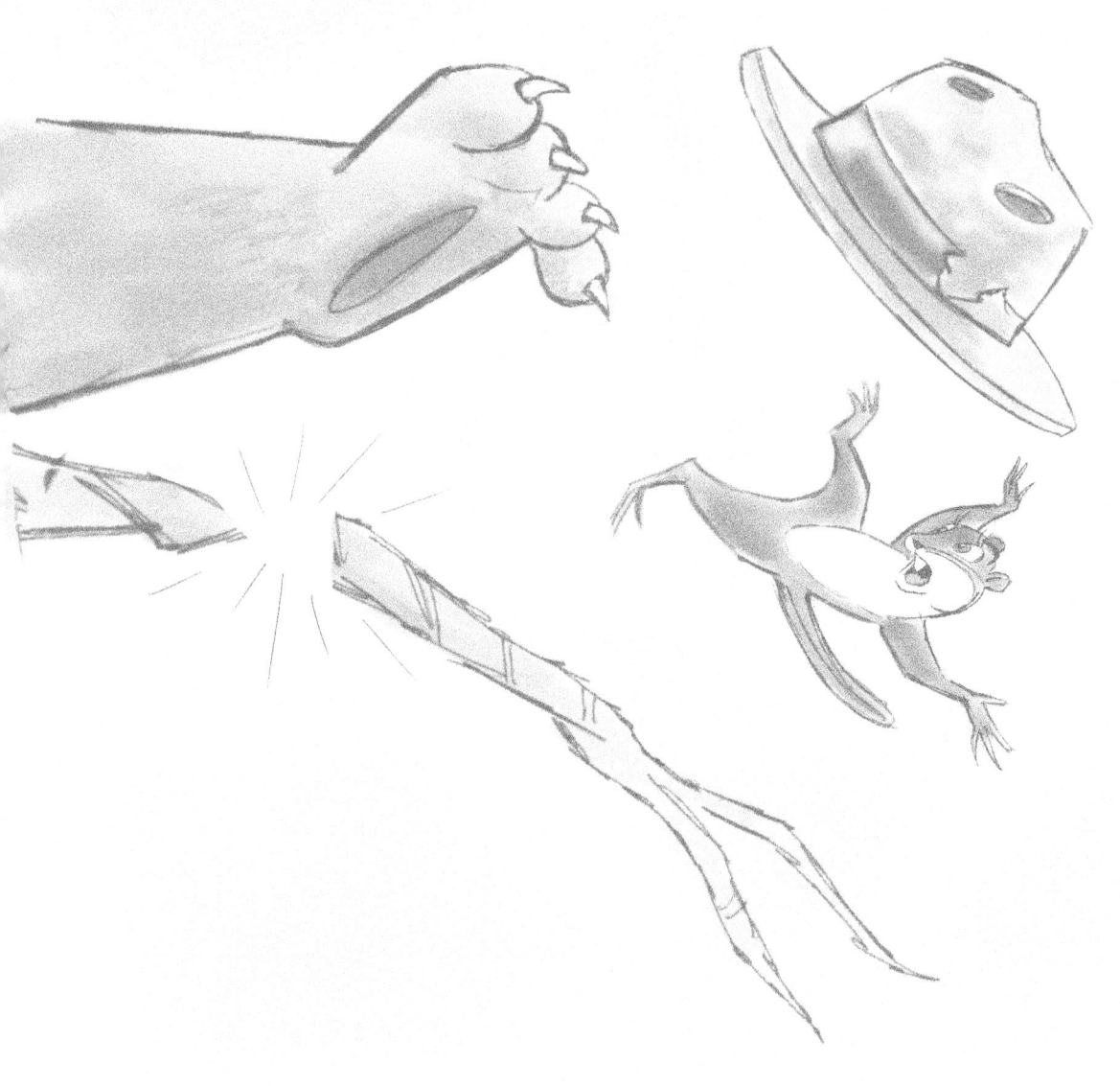

Parents and Young Readers

Children intuitively believe they can learn to read. Parents support their children in their reading journey by fostering this inborn belief and confidence, especially during their early reading years (between ages 4-8). Providing reading materials that include predictable patterns is an easy way to encourage young readers. Many early reading books use patterns, such as rhyming words, alliteration, counting, or the alphabet. Our brains search for patterns because patterns make sense.

When children recognize a pattern and complete it for themselves, their confidence soars. Increased confidence fuels a child's drive to read and lays the foundation for future reading.

It is well known that reading patterned and other books to young children builds a foundation for future success as a reader. Less known is the power of dictation. When children dictate to their parents their language about an art project or any event in their life, they learn that the words they speak are the same words authors put into books. This dictated language becomes a source of reading material for parents to read back to their children later.

Wordless Books for Young Authors magnify this dictation process by providing a whole book for children to dictate and later read back to others. Adults can either write directly in the book or purchase 3" x 7" labels to print and place in the book. When children see their own words in a book and can read them back to an audience their confidence grows.

Children must maintain their confidence to hear themselves read a book at the same pace, with the same voice inflections and pauses as an adult. Using wordless books and dictation builds this confidence and empowers children to read their own ideas. They will proudly read to family, friends, and grandparents. The process of learning to read should be so painless that children forget how they learned to read, yet the stories are so powerful they are remembered for life.

www.ingramcontent.com/pod-product-compliance
Lightning Source LLC
Chambersburg PA
CBHW041530120626
46551CB00018B/2644